DAMAGED BUT NOT DESTROYED

A Story of Forgiveness, Faith, and Favour

Julene Grant-Percy

www.hcpbookpublishing.com

ISBN-13: 978-1-958404-34-8 (paperback)

Unless otherwise stated, all Scripture quotations are taken
from the KJV.

DEDICATION

To broken women, women who believe they have no hope, women who are hurting, and Christian women wearing their salvation and Christian offices as cloaks for their hurt, this book is dedicated to you.

To my mom, Dorothy Gordon-Thompson.

ACKNOWLEDGMENTS

Without doubt, I acknowledge, salute, and glorify the Lord and Saviour of my life, Jesus Christ, the Lord, without whom this book would not have been possible.

I acknowledge my mentor and bishop, Apostle Richard. A. McKenzie, who has been a tower of strength, praying for and encouraging me on this Christian journey.

I bless God for my mother, who is my friend and confidant, who took very good care of me, her only daughter. She is one of my biggest supporters, and she has stood with me in ministry and is one of my cheerleaders.

Thanks to Rev. Valentine Rodney for his invaluable contribution to the success of this project.

I would like to acknowledge and wish the best for every individual who was mentioned in this book, for without them, my journey would not have been the testimony it is.

Leo is a gift sent from God. I believe the Lord intentionally sent him as a destiny helper in my life. He helped me with this book, and I am grateful.

Thanks to the members of the Healing Our Women family who have been with me for over five years. They have stood with me in prayer and encouraged me in the times when everything did not seem to be coming together. I am extremely grateful for their sacrifices and prayers.

TABLE OF CONTENTS

Dedication... iii

Acknowledgements v

Foreword 9

Endorsements 13

Prologue... 19

Preface 21

Damaged! 23

Chapter 1: Growing (not) in Grace 25

Chapter 2: May Pen to Granny 31

Chapter 3: "I'm Out" 45

Chapter 4: "Soup! Soup!" 57

Not Destroyed! 65

Chapter 5: Salvation at last 67

Chapter 6: "Have the very Faith of God!" 83

Chapter 7: Forgiveness, Faith and Favour!........... 107

Epilogue... 117

Author Biography.. 119

References 121

FOREWORD

This book, "Damaged But Not Destroyed," gives the reader an insight, not only into the life and culture of a Jamaican upbringing, but also presents a keen insight into the life's journey of Julene. You will come face to face with the thoughts, life, dreams, and aspirations of a young girl who morphed into the struggles and dangers of adulthood; years that ultimately culminated into the most defining moment of her life when she came to faith in Christ. It presents an opportunity for both ministry and healing, especially for hurting women. The real question presented is not whether God can help you but whether you will receive and embrace His help. It is about transformation and, indeed, hope for the hurting. It demonstrates how to experience real-life change despite the dramas of life. While we will agree that the Julene's journey continues, we see the hand of the Master Potter restoring a vessel that was damaged but not ultimately destroyed.

This narrative will arrest your attention, and you will see both the power and consequences of decision-making. It portrays the fact that life can be altered or shaped simply by the choices we make or the effects that the choices of others would have on the outcome of our lives.

There is, however, a deeper message that presents itself as the story unfolds: that no life is beyond the power of redemptive grace. The main hero is not Julene, but the Lord Jesus Christ, whose unparalleled love for her became both her source of strength and ultimate point of refuge and salvation. It was God's timely interventions that repeatedly rescued her from a far worse fate than the trajectory her life would have taken her on.

Julene takes us as passengers on a journey that is not for the faint of heart. Through the twists and turns, we find ourselves reliving her story but being extremely thankful that she would ultimately yield to God's amazing grace. This is not just telling a story but rather presenting life lessons. It is far better to learn from her experiences than to suffer the fate of poor decision-making.

God not only healed and transformed her but has placed her in a position to both minister and serve His people in various capacities. Her launching of various ministries (for example, HOW) and initiatives (for example, Feeding Programme) is a testimony that God not only heals but will use you to help those trapped in the very places He delivered you from.

This book is a tool for ministry and transformation. You will see a loving and forgiving God who will never hold our past against us. You will see the resilience of faith and the faithfulness of God to redeem and bless not because of who we are but despite who we are.

No matter how marred the clay was in the Potter's hand, He did not dispose of it but rather reshaped and refashioned it. There is still hope for the discouraged and hurting.

Rev. Valentine Rodney

Author and Educator

ENDORSEMENTS

Apostle Julene Percy has unmasked and shown us in this book that God can heal and use broken vessels, if we are willing and obedient. This book is a testament of the journey of a woman who dared to take the risk of serving a God she would come to know. As I read through the chapters of this book, I see the life of a person who has been transformed by the power of the Holy Spirit. This book reveals a story of trials and triumph and of how God takes us through the process of life and brings us into purpose. I really believe this book will be a blessing to the masses and will ultimately bring deliverance to those who are bound by the power of the enemy.

I must say that not many persons are willing to unveil and let you see their scars, nakedness, and vulnerabilities, but Apostle Julene has exposed her flaws, faults, and insecurities so that those who may dare to read this book may receive freedom. *Damaged But Not Destroyed* will bless your life, and I, as an apostle and author, gladly endorse this book. Amen.

Apostle Nadine Forrest

Spiritual Mother

Julene heard the voice of God calling her that Wednesday mid-morning, saying "Daughter! Come unto Me," and Julene's heart answered "Yes Lord! I am coming."

As I interacted with her, I knew there was something supernatural about the anointing on her life and that such an anointing came with several gifts of the Spirit; the mighty and heavenly calling on her life was massive. She would rapidly move on, like the woman at the well who met Jesus, to run and call others "Come see a man named Jesus Christ of Nazareth, the Life-giver and Healer."

Today, her ministries are touching the hopeless and homeless, women and men, girls and boys who have lost their way and are engulfed in the trap of fear and dread brought on by deception, family curses, un-forgiveness, and anger, amongst so many destructive elements set up by Satan. Her ministry is growing by leaps and bounds, and her voice continues to echo throughout the earth reaching the ears and hearts of the lost, damaged and destroyed, bidding them to "Come see this Man Christ Jesus of Nazareth" who gave her life more abundantly and will do likewise for them.

I highly endorse this book, and I believe it will change your life forever. This book is a reflection of Christ's gifts of hope, peace, forgiveness of sin and love, amongst so many other attributes of which humanity should taste. *Damaged But Not Destroyed* will open your eyes to Julene's story of forgiveness, faith and favour and comes highly endorsed by the Holy Spirit.

God bless you as you read.

Shalom! Shalom!

Dr. Loretta Sewell-Drummond

D. Psych. MA, BA, Dip. Sp. Ed. Dip. Th.

First, I would like to thank our Lord and Saviour, Jesus Christ, for giving Apostle Julene Percy so much grace, compassion, and love for His precious children.

Apostle Julene is known to me for over twenty years, and during that time, I found her to be an amazing Spirit-filled woman of God. She is faithful, hardworking, devoted, committed, and dedicated to her calling. She sincerely loves the work of God and working for His people.

Apostle Percy has grown tremendously in the Word of God, in prayer, in faith, wisdom and in the ministry of the prophetic. I have read Apostle Julene book "Damaged But Not Destroyed" and it is a book that is designed to bring healing and complete restoration to the hearts of men. She is heavily anointed, and her powerful book is geared to motivate people's faith to have a closer, deeper encounter with Christ.

I was blown away by how her book was written and divinely structured, and what amazes me is how the anointing keeps spilling from page to page, even toward the end. I believe God is the one who has inspired this book, and because of it, many persons will receive their blessings.

This book gives you the courage to firmly hold to the truth of Christ Jesus and keep close to calvary's cross. Apostle Percy's inspiring story in the ministry has left an indelible impact on the lives of thousands of people around the world. She is indeed a great leader and one to aspire and follow.

I have considered Apostle's life to be a one-of-a-kind book that you can't stop but read for the enriching, enlightening, and solid documentation it entails. Her life in Christ captures the hearts of men and motivates them to serve God willingly and sincerely. Apostle's life in the faith of our Lord Jesus Christ matches the amazing love that she has for the service of God. She is one who is relatable wherever she goes, and Apostle possesses the wisdom, knowledge, and insight of God. Apostle Percy travels far and near to do the work of God, and nothing stops her from getting the work done; again, I say she stops at nothing!

I have seen and heard of countless testimonies coming from her ministry and what the Lord has done for many of His people to whom she ministers worldwide.

Apostle Percy has been a blessing to me and also to my ministry. She was raised with prophets at an early age in her ministry and long before she gave her heart to Jesus. She had a good foundation which makes her deeply rooted and grounded.

Apostle Percy, I am so proud of you and what God is doing in and through your life, and also what He is about to do.

I have endorsed this book and recommend it to everyone, both saved and unsaved alike, because it has no boundaries to the category of people it can reach worldwide. I urge you, the reader, to introduce this book to everyone around you, and let them know that it's a must-read book.

May this book be printed in different languages, and may it be a blessing wherever it goes, in Jesus' name.

Bishop R.A. McKenzie

Author

PROLOGUE

"Strength and honour are her clothing; and she shall rejoice in time to come." (Proverbs 31:25).

"The just shall live by faith." (Romans 1:17c).

PREFACE

After hosting several Healing Our Women (HOW) conferences, I became more aware of the countless number of women who have suffered various forms of abuse. These conferences, therefore, became points of contact between God and these hurting women. The purpose of this book is to strengthen women, like me, who have suffered traumatic experiences. It is not my intent to make excuses for the decisions we as women make, and which we may pay for, but to highlight how a damaged life can still be victorious when struggles are used as God's process to perfection in Christ; a process that liberates us from sin and its damaging and devastating effects.

My life is a testament to Jesus' ability and proclivity to heal the wounds and scars that hurt has dealt us, if we humbly surrender to Him in faith. The Lord has impressed upon me, time and time again, to pen my story (bits of it anyway), for the purpose of encouraging women across the globe. I believe it will inspire and heal women who have been struggling and suffering; women who are in need of God's touch; women who are on the brink of destruction.

The Lord was present, even though not evident to me, for every incident, hurt, struggle, heartache, and pain that I suffered, even though many of them occurred because of poor decision-making on my part. But He took these situations and transformed them into the pieces of a process puzzle, vehicles of and for my maturation, because He was more than capable of working them together for my good (see Romans 8:28).

In the chapters that follow, I will unfold my journey and demonstrate that God's faith and favour came hand in hand with His plan of salvation and forgiveness for me, and no doubt it is the same for us all.

Be blessed.

DAMAGED!

A *wah dis mi get miself inna though, God?[1]*

Here I was, heading to what was certain doom, and maybe my tomb; being held against my will by a man whom I once called lover. We had confessed our love for each other, to each other, on many occasions prior, but now, I was being kidnapped, terrifyingly staring death in the face, and death's hand was that of my lover, or more accurately, that of my "ex-lover." You see, he cheated on me, so, I thought it fair game to move on with my life—find someone else and call it quits on this already illicit affair. After all, he already had a significant other in his life, or possibly significant others; some of them maybe younger than I was. What was happening? My life was going great: I was good-looking and had the body of an athlete; I owned a car; lived in a gated community; had all my bills paid on time, every time; and dined in style whenever I wanted. And now, I'm bargaining for my life, inside my own car no less.

"God help me!!!"

---

[1] "What is this that I have gotten myself into, God?"

CHAPTER 1

GROWING (NOT) IN GRACE

I drew my first breaths in my great-grandmother's house in Palmer's Cross, Clarendon, and here, my cries would fill the halls and walls of another granny's house, at least for a while. In some way, the circumstances surrounding my birth, though lacklustre, were almost prophetic: grandparents, and family, would leave indelible marks on my life, physically, emotionally, and spiritually, and additionally, play an undeniably significant role in who I was to become; in what I have become.

My early years in May Pen were short-lived however, because subsequently, we: my mother, brother and I, left Clarendon to live in St. Ann courtesy of an invitation from my mother's aunt (another grand; Benty was her name). As it relates to education, we: my brother and I, were enrolled in the Discovery Bay All-Age School, which I attended up until the second grade. School was ordinary, or so I would classify it, and the activities I engaged in were indicative of the regimen of a normal Jamaican primary school. I went to school, listened to the teacher, wrote what the teachers wrote, and played with friends. You could say that I was just along for the ride or simply going through the motions.

My mother was a clothing merchant, and she would travel to countries abroad procuring clothing, which she later sold in the Brown's Town marketplace upon her return. This made her frequently absent from home. The job of oversight, therefore, would fall to my aunt, Auntie Sharon, mom's youngest sister, while mom was away. Auntie Sharon was kind, sweet and, I would think, self-sacrificing oftentimes. She would come to Discovery Bay all the way from May Pen to fulfil her babysitting duties. She never stopped supporting or helping me. I would end up spending almost all (if not all) of my final year at Vere Technical High School living with her. My family is a family of cooks, and Auntie Sharon was truly a member of the family: a very good cook.

Deceitfully and Disobediently Discovering the Bay

The mundane rigour of school aside, I enjoyed living in Discovery Bay. Which child wouldn't? After all, the beach was just a stone's throw away, and I *loved* the sea, regardless of the blissfully souring *aftermath* of enjoying an entire day of swimming. My mother forbade swimming though, and rightly so. Her warnings, however, were no deterrent for a girl who repeatedly went back to the sea, although her stepsister had to save her from drowning on one occasion, an ordeal that should have taught her the lesson that her mother tried to spank into her every time she found evidence of the water world escapades. The beach was my home away from home; like the threat of drowning was going to stop me from submerging my little *tuccus* in that glorious body of water.

Disobedient? Yup! Guilty as charged. I guess I epitomized Proverbs 22:15, so to speak.

Yes, my mother warned and whooped me for my disobedience. We (me, my brother, and my stepsister) were young, and we often visited the beach unsupervised; ergo the need for the warnings. But, like any set of disobedient children, we went nonetheless, and when we returned, we concealed the evidence (*or we tried to conceal the evidence*). We would hide our drenched clothing under our mattresses hoping that mommy would not find them or not notice the water on the floor beneath; she always did. But, the *aftermath*, the unquestionable evidence, even more so, could not be concealed;

those tattletales would not be silenced; those EYES of mine; those bloodshot, sea-bitten eyes always told on me, and so did my hair.

I couldn't hide my beach outings because, additionally, I returned home with half the sand from the beach (I exaggerate, of course) between and among the strands of my kinky, unprocessed hair. My mother would kunk[2] me in the head with the comb while she washed and combed it, feverishly trying to remove the grains of sand. I would have kunked me too, DWL. But, if almost drowning didn't stop me from going to the beach, what was a kunk or two from my mother? Those were my Discovery Bay days: school, beach and a couple of kunks in the head. Those (in)gloriously rebellious days.

I was a bit accident prone as well (as if the almost drowning didn't clue you in). Of course, I could go into details about spilling boiled water from a stove on my foot, or about the time I was running, and a barbed wire fence almost took one of my eyes, each situation warranting a visit to the hospital. This all happened while living with my grandparents; however, all in all, I came out fine by the mercy and grace of God.

---

[2] Slight knocks in the head (reprimand; not abuse)

The way God provided for and preserved me leads me to surmise that sometimes, if not all the time, God's purpose is open for all to see, even the devil. I am grateful that even though disobedient to my mother and her dictates, the Lord, through the people around me, who were also conduits of his favour, helped to preserve my life to the fulfilment of purpose. This is what I now try to communicate in this book—to God, your purpose is paramountly more important than your past. My purpose would have drowned if not for my stepsister: there would not have been a Healing Our Women Conference; I would not be an apostle, preaching the gospel of Christ; I would not have had two beautiful children of my own; this book would not have been penned. His provision would extend even beyond my immediate family in the person of my stepfather.

Stepfather: Framing Fatherhood

It was in Discovery Bay that my mother caught the eye of the man who would become my stepfather, and this book would not be complete without mentioning his contribution to my life. His actions reorganized and reframed my understanding of fatherhood. I did not have a good relationship with my real father at that time. Case in point, when my brother and I had to go back to Clarendon to live with my grandparents—my mother was still living in Discovery Bay—we would always take the long trip through the winding roads that went through Chapelton, Trout Hall, Cave Valley, Brown's Town and, finally, Discovery Bay, to be with them both. He would ensure that we were well taken care of during our short visits, and that our return to Clarendon was eased and sweetened with a few extra dollars in our pockets. I can't think of anything that he did wrong, or if he did, I did not know about it. I can't recall him exhibiting any aggression toward us either. I am very grateful for his commitment to fostering me.

Visiting Discovery Bay to be with mom during the Christmas season was a bomb. The Brown's Town marketplace became our playground on Christmas Eve, and we would spend the entire night walking the streets of Brown's Town while mom sold her goods throughout the night into Christmas morning. Returning to May Pen to live became permanent. We would return to live with our grandparents (to an abusive grandfather), who owned an old house situated on Chapelton Road, and, like Revelation says, "there would be no more sea" for me. My brother would later migrate to Barbados, leaving me alone with my grandparents and their other grandchildren.

CHAPTER 2

MAY PEN TO GRANNY

Fatherhood

While living in May Pen, my biological father offered my mother and I very little support, and neither did we, my father and I, have a relationship to speak of, even though he lived and worked in May Pen. According to my mother, he had flatly denied paternity at one point. Our interactions were basically centered on me lying in wait for him at the May Pen taxi stand, in the immediate vicinity of the Dr. Bell Memorial clock tower, to furnish me with lunch money, or just even to get a lift to school. He was a taxi driver. On several occasions, I went away from the taxi stand empty-handed. One could only imagine my disappointment. After a while, it did not matter though; I had grown accustomed to it. Such was our *relationship*.

Paul, in his letter to Timothy, addressed the problem of the irresponsible father, and as dogmatic and damning as it sounds, he states that such an individual is worse than an unbeliever (1 Timothy 5:8). To liken a father of that nature to someone who doesn't believe in Christ is like saying that irresponsible fathers (one who does not see to the affairs of his family) is worthy of hell fire. I don't think my father knew this, though. You could say my life almost began with its foundations "built upon the sand," characterized by the oh-so-common sociological phenomena of poverty and the absentee biological father that came to define the state of many Jamaican families in that era. But thank the Lord God for salvation! We now have a better relationship, and he is now sweetly saved and living for the Lord; a very active Seventh-Day Adventist, if I might add.

School, Sports, and Grandma

While living in May Pen, I was enrolled in the Osbourne Store All-Age School—now Osbourne Store Junior High—and then Vere Technical High School. I was not naturally intelligent, but I was very athletic, and while attending Osbourne Store All-Age, I participated in all forms of track and field events, the long jump being my best event. I was so good that I represented Clarendon in the country's inter-parish competitions, and my talents would see me being headhunted by Vere Technical High school's track and field team; a team which, at the time, was the island's premiere ISSA Girls Athletics Championships winner. As a matter of fact, they won the girls' championships during the periods of 1967-

32

1968, 1974-1975, and then 1979-1993[3]–a total of nineteen years; a dynasty and powerhouse of the girls' champs if there ever was one. So, you can imagine my elation when I was drafted. Unfortunately (or fortunately), while attending Vere, my performances fell short of what was required or expected to become a main competitor for the school, so I concentrated my energies on other activities, specifically the cadet corps and netball.

I was an excellent goalkeeper and was selected to train with Jamaica's national under-21 squad, along with my then friends, Georgina Hibbert and Samantha "Kelly" Robinson. Disappointments ensued, but the Lord ALWAYS knows best. My grandmother objected to the regimen that I would have been subjected to while training for the national team, as vying to represent the country at this level meant that I had to attend training sessions every Saturday in Kingston, and my grandmother told me that it was out of the question. I was rebellious and loved the company of boys, so maybe they didn't

---

[3] The Gleaner Company. 2022. Past winners of ISSA/GraceKennedy Boys and Girls' Championships. 5 April. Accessed July 22, 2022. https://jamaica-gleaner.com/article/sports/20220405/past-winners-issagracekennedy-boys-and-girls-championships.

trust me either. Reflecting on it now, I couldn't blame her.

My Saturdays were church-centric: chores and activities were all about preparing for church the next morning (so netball practice was a no-no). I still remember washing my clothes with a form of cake soap called *dutty gyal* in the Jamaican vernacular and straightening my clothes with coal-stove-heated iron. DWL! I thank God for these experiences because if they hadn't instilled the importance of God in my life, I am not sure who I would be today. I think I could attribute my understanding of true church culture to the nurturing principles afforded by the practices associated with my Saturday regimen, all enforced by my grandmother. I didn't like them one bit, but I had to do them.

Church was not the only reason why netball took a back seat. I had examinations to consider as well, and, as I said, I wasn't a bright student. At the time, I was pursuing four CXC subjects at the fifth form level, and I knew it would take a miracle to succeed in all four, but I wanted to prove to my detractors, my step-grandfather especially, that I was somebody after all, and that I could amount to something. I wanted to prove that I wasn't some pretty dunce. So,

I did the only thing I knew how to: I wrote the Lord a letter. I do not recall all the details, but I clearly remember the overall sentiment and intent: "Lord, help me to pass two of these subjects," and all glory to God in the highest, I did. I ended up with passes in Home Management and Food and Nutrition; I told you that my family was a family of cooks.

This feat wasn't easy however, because I had to study without the aid of electricity; using a kerosene fuelled lamp to read my notes and textbooks. My childhood was riddled with these seemingly unfortunate experiences. One such experience is the ritual hair washing, done using *Sudsil* as my all-in-one shampoo and conditioner. Sudsil was a white powdered detergent, packaged in a small carton box decorated with yellow and red swirls—one of the most advertised at the time. What are you going to do when you cannot afford shampoo? Jamaica's lower and lower-middle class demographic would not experience the bliss that accompanied the use of the technological advances of the day; Jamaica had been awarded her independence just over two decades ago. Yes, we were poor; Dr. Suds provided the shampoo, and a lamp was my light bulb.

Sunday

My Sundays were no party. After coming from a long, arduous service—Sunday School, Divine worship— I had to begin another bout of preparation; I had school on Monday. My uniforms needed ironing, and using that horrifyingly heavy self-heater iron was the least among the travesties (of course, again, I exaggerate) I had to endure on Sunday evenings: every Sunday evening, I had to iron three of my cousins' uniforms as well. Sometimes I had to wait until after the ration of a meal was done cooking to heat the second coal-heated iron on grandma's stove. "This is unfair," I often thought. "Why do I have to iron their clothes? Why can't they do it themselves?" Truth be told, they couldn't have done it themselves anyway; they were too young and too small.

I appreciated being at church because of the social interactions, not so much because of what church really was. I am not sure if I fully understood what church was about either. I understood it to be a meeting place of sorts where I interacted with my peers in a wholesome environment; an environment filled with activities I had to participate in, and I was in everything. Sunday school and Sunday school choir, youth, prayer meeting, vacation Bible school;

36

you name it, I was in it. There was absolutely nothing I could have excused myself from, not when my grandmother was one of the prominent church mothers. To this day, I can still recall standing and repeating my Sunday school golden texts.

On a different note, the church mothers captured my attention and admiration. They often dressed in white for church and sang fervently in worship to the Lord. To this day, I still minister in a white dress (sometimes) when I am asked to preach at a church.

My grandmother planted the seed alright. She even taught me what praying was. She was an ardent prayer warrior and a faithful participating member of her church, and those traits captured my admiration. Her early morning M.O. was characterized by hours of prayer, calling the names of her children and grandchildren to the Lord. I guess this was where I learnt, if even just by her practice, the how-tos of intercession. Later, after my conversion, I would have the privilege of accompanying great prayer warriors in the persons of Pastor Elaine Holness and Missionary Wint to various prayer meetings. My grandmother was the driving force behind my attendance at church and my exposure to the things of God, but not only.

Tough Times

Looking back at the situation, it could not have been easy for my grandparents. They had to take care of nine of us, children and grandchildren alike, and we were poor. So, you can imagine the size of dinner given the fact that I would often get "short-changed" by my step-grandfather. Even sadder still, my grandmother was an excellent cook. My appetite would only be opened with her cooking just for me to be let down because the food was so little. Saturday was soup day, and I loved, and I mean loved, her beef-bone soup. We could only afford the bone to make soup (it's a Jamaican thing), but to me, regardless, it was the best soup I had ever tasted in my entire life. All her wonderful meals were cooked by a coal stove; we could not afford gas much less a gas fuelled stove. We had what we had; it was tough, but grandma made it work; she made us work.

We did not escape working around the house, so if there was anything to be done, it was a chore— washing dishes on a sheet of zinc on the outside, starting a coal fire for dinner, and any job they thought we could manage at our various ages and stages. On various occasions, these chores were monitored by a disciplinarian aunt. We, the children, welcomed her presence as much as the Radcliffe's

38

welcomed Cruella Deville to their house (101 Dalmatians), as much as one would welcome stray wild goats at a wedding, but we could do nothing to prevent her visiting. She was such a disciplinarian. Oh my God, Aunt Elaine! Whenever she came to the house, the first thing on her agenda was a top-to-bottom cleaning of the house before we had anything to eat. It seems then that, for her and inevitably for us, eating was only a reward for hard work—if you don't work, you don't eat.

Part of her regimen was to walk the floors barefooted after we had swept and polished it, feeling for any particles of dirt or polish residue on the floor. If she felt anything under her feet other than what she thought was the smooth, slippery surface of a well-polished floor, then the floor wasn't clean, so, our plates would remain clean (free of food) until we got it right. Can you imagine how disgruntled and perturbed we were as children, having had to soldier through the navy seal-like regimen for cleaning a floor? First, it was swept with a thatched broom, then polished by applying the floor polish with some kind of cloth, and finally shined with the husk of a dried coconut that was cut in half to make a brush (a coconut brush). We hated those hours.

Grandma taught me quite a bit. Many of the skills I learnt about shopping in the market came from her. I still recall going to the market on a Saturday morning and watching her choose her goods and picking specific vendors from which to buy. Because she always looked for the best products, I too became vigilant in my selection of food products. I guess, in some way, I was led to do food and nutrition through grandma. And why not? Sunday meals were like sweet roller-coaster rides for my tastebuds; callaloo and fried dumplings with chocolate tea for breakfast and dinner was free-range chicken—what we Jamaicans call *common fowl*—done in any style grandma chose. My tastebuds rejoiced, but my teeth could not sink into the bones of those common fowls; I would need special equipment for that.

I loved grandma's cooking, but I hated her house— the first house at least—and I was embarrassed to live there. I couldn't invite my friends over to visit me in that rickety old wooden structure that I called home, let alone the embarrassment I would face if they needed to use the toilet, at which point, I would have to direct them to the *outhouse of horrors* (pit toilet). That smelly roach-infested monstrosity was the subject of many nightmare-like moments for me, moments which now bring me to a hilarious fit of laughter.

It wasn't a perfect life, and I did not do much to make it better. I used to steal away from the house to go to the bottom of the road to hang out and chat with the boys in the community. The conversations proved exciting, and I found them, the boys, not just the conversations, fun to be around. Not to mention, I had a liking for one of them.

"Abuse? How Could I Have Known?"

My step-grandfather's parenting skills didn't help to correct or improve my behaviour either. For starters, grandma suffered much physical abuse at his hand, and so did I. On one occasion, he slapped me across my face so intensely that I saw *mini-mini*[4]. To add insult to injury, he would often share my dinner, and it would be recognizably less in comparison to his children and grandchildren. I would often tell my grandmother of his abuse, and she always defended me, but her defense fell on his obstinate ears; I guess that was just who he was. At the time, I didn't know

---

[4] A Jamaican phrase for the flashes of light of varying sizes, which occupy one's field of vision for different periods of time, a result of stress to the nerves in the retina.

that how he treated me was classified as abuse. Maybe the phenomenon of child abuse was not yet invented or even reached a third-world Jamaica. What I did know was that this current form of treatment was markedly dissimilar from what I learnt from my stepfather. I just knew how it felt, physically and emotionally, and even though he was a good provider, a mechanic by trade, he still had his issues; issues which would see my grandmother and I suffering because of them.

There were other forms of abuse, and back then, they seemed to have been the norm, and being that I was disobedient, or as Jamaicans would say "ears-hard," I was constantly *disciplined*. There were times when I was beaten so badly that abrasions were left on my skin. I was lashed with tamarind branches, told that I would amount to nothing, and missed opportunities in school. The feelings of loathing and rejection were real. When your parents, grandparents or any form of authoritative figure tells you that you would not amount to anything good, which is what I was told, you tend to take it as it is. You may not have agreed with the statement, or worse yet, you were locked into the emotional trauma or shock that the abuse placed you in that you did nothing about the utterance which was made over your life, and whether you understood it or not, the words lingered, waiting on someone or something to fulfil it.

It was almost so.

CHAPTER 3

"I'M OUT"

"Thank God!"

Out of Granny's House

Finally, I was old enough to hightail it out of my grandparents' house. Now, I would be accountable and answerable to no one; a *rebel with a cause*. I was a long way from Discovery Bay, and it was a long time since those ill-advised illicit beach excursions, but the heart of the rebel pounded vivaciously in my chest, bringing life to my being. I was rife with self-will. This was my chance to get away, and I did.

I really didn't like living with my grandparents anyway, despite learning so much from my grandmother. So, getting out of that house was, to me, a gift from God (even though He might have had nothing to do with it). No more roaches! After all, I was old enough to be on my own, to make my own decisions, and not to mention the relief of avoiding a *serving of backhand* handed to me for what I thought was no apparent reason or wrongdoing. NO MORE *MINI-MINI*! I was free!

Not long after graduating from Vere Technical, subjects in hand and overjoyed for making the graduation list, I walked out of my grandparents' house and walked straight into my boyfriend's (not immediately, but you get the gist). He loved me, and I loved him (I thought); hey, if I was going to do this (leave grandma, I mean), who better to be on my own with? Ironically, his house was his mother's house.

I could not have predicted the occurrences or mishaps that would later terrify me, cause me comparably more emotional turmoil than I had experienced before, and even threaten my very existence. I could not have predicted my journey, and maybe if I was closer to the Lord, He would have revealed my comeuppances to me before they happened and, possibly, through His favour, given me a way of escape. Because whether we know it or not, He does know the plans He has for us (see Jeremiah 29:11), and He does provide a means of escape from the enemy's traps (see 1 Corinthians 10:13). Thankfully, it was not all a downward spiral, because the Lord threw in a blessing here and there, and allowed me, with some level of comfort, to enjoy some semblance of a good life. By saying "good life," I do not mean that how I was living was essentially good by scripture's definition. It simply means that I had some blessings along the way.

My boyfriend was a nice guy; he treated me very well, and I had no complaints. He was affectionate, loving, caring, and all those niceties a girl could want (assuming I knew what all girls wanted), but I cheated on him. There was nothing wrong with our relationship, and I still don't know or remember if there was a reason why I cheated. What was I looking for? Was I missing something? There are some who would argue that maybe he did not fulfil my needs, but that couldn't have been the case because, as I said, *he did nothing wrong*.

My indiscretion, however, and consequently, led to the birth of my two children—my dearest blessings. Solomon writes: "*Lo, children are an heritage of the Lord: and the fruit of the womb is His reward.*" (Psalm 127:3). You see, God has a way of encouraging us while we are in error, so, even though I went in the wrong direction, my children may have been sources of encouragement. Of course, this is in no wise a reason to sin, but I am grateful to the Lord for my children.

It is through these blessings that Paul's writing can be firmly understood. In his letter to the Romans, he wrote, "*But God commendeth His love toward us, in that, while we were yet sinners, Christ died for us.*" (Romans 5:8). The term "toward" suggests an act or process—God has begun, done and continues to perform a series or a set of love-inspired, love-initiated, and love-infused actions that influences or dictates our lived experiences, each of these experiences working for our good (see Romans 8:28). Jesus' sacrifice is not only an atonement for sin to the Most High (who is angry at sin), but a demonstration of love on His part towards the said sinner—He became sin so that we could become God's righteousness (see 2 Corinthians 5:21). I was in sin, but Jesus made my children a reflection of His promised blessing toward me. Even though they are backslidden, they are very much a part of my life and I pray for their return to the Lord; after all, they are *His* reward, and their return to the straight and narrow will be His re-reward.

The other side of that coin is a requirement on the part of the intended recipient, the sinner, to begin their own series of actions, His love to receive. But I didn't place myself in the position to receive it in the manner that mattered: *repent, confess belief in the*

Lord Jesus Christ and baptism for the remission of sin. Mind you, I liked the social activities church came with and enjoyed being among God's people— the fellowship, the love, the praise—but sadly, the object of my love was not the One who deserved it most.

Chapelton Road, Again

So, I cheated on my *high school sweetheart*, got pregnant, and without a doubt, I was no longer welcome in his mother's house. "Where do I go from here?" Or even more troubling "Where do I live?" As you might have imagined, I did the next best thing; the best of the evils: I went back to granny (so much for getting out). Here I was, with child, going back to the place where I had so happily left; to the place where I had faced much ridicule. But what else was I supposed to do? I would face even more ridicule now given the fulfilment of "turning out to nothing" becoming evident from my burgeoning belly and cradle-like pelvis and hips, all accompanied by a vacant unadorned left ring finger (Did my grandfather see my future?). Regardless of all the negative thoughts churning in my mind, God gave me favour, and my grandmother was gracious enough to receive me. The shame of returning to Chapelton Road was further abated because my new living arrangements included spending half the time with my daughter's father; it was better than spending the entire time with my grandmother; my step-grandfather, sadly, had passed.

Motherhood

Two years after giving birth to my daughter, I enrolled with HEART Academy (now HEART NSTA) in Runaway Bay, St. Ann, where I majored in Food and Nutrition. One of the benefits of the program was that it allowed me to learn and earn. Students were placed in jobs locally and given a chance to earn foreign exchange through their work and travel program—the overseas component. I worked in Nantucket in that regard, but I became *blue* and homesick: I was missing my daughter. Don't get me wrong, I enjoyed the experience, but after six months, I was missing my baby. I additionally foiled the opportunity as well by getting into an altercation with one of the staff members while working at the restaurant that hired me, and they never asked me to return. I guess silver linings are never without their share of dark clouds.

The love for my daughter (or maybe the fire in my fists) sealed my fate. I came back to Jamaica to be with my baby and her father. We: my child's father and I, would find it too easy, it would seem, to get into rifts. One evening we had an argument that would find us hastening to the hospital. I fell and broke my left ankle, and now, I would be down for the count for months to come. Maybe we were missing the softer responses necessary to quell our arguments (see Proverbs 15:1). He wasn't afraid of picking up the slack during this period—doing the chores, taking care of the baby, etc.—and that was a great relief. He was, and still is, a very good father.

At three years of age, my daughter developed a hernia, and her paediatrician recommended early surgery. I was a bit concerned but it was nothing major, and the surgery was done in a day. Later, I welcomed my son into the world. He was a big boy, approximately ten pounds, so he was delivered via a Caesarean section (C-Section). The recovery process was extremely problematic, but Aunt Sharon would come to the rescue. I spent two weeks with her while I recovered from the operation. His father, also my daughter's father, was in England at the time of his birth, and they didn't meet until a few years ago. When he planned his return, a short visit of course, I planned the reunion between them as a surprise: "I'm going to the airport to pick someone up." It had been seventeen years since he left, and the road was not easy at all. His visit, however, was filled with joy; a truly emotion-filled moment for all.

Even though he was not physically present for all those years, my children and I felt his love from across the Atlantic. He supported them financially, and we were very rarely in need. His phone calls came in like clockwork, and very often, he kept close contact with them. I think I can safely say that the manner in which he conducted himself toward us is tantamount to him being with us physically. He even bought a bus which he licensed as a public passengers' vehicle; another source of income for his family. He gave them so much support, and I thank God for who he is.

It was not easy raising the kids alone while he was away (even though his support was clear and evident). For one, my son had a little bit of trouble; well, by today's standards, but he was a boy. There was more to him than sitting down around desks and studying for hours on end without anywhere to focus his pent-up energy. Teachers would often report that he was always on the outside of the school kicking bottles and what-not. When he had to sit his grade four test, he requested that I pray for him before I left the school, and that I did. There was nothing wrong with this little man of mine; he was hyperactive, and I bless God that he is who he is.

A Different Kind of Romeo

Eventually, I met another man. I thought he was the world to me, but that is the nature of relationships— while in the moment, the individual becomes your world. He furnished me with all my needs, and I was okay with that. I lived in a gated community and I was living the dream. I had what I needed and what I wanted. I guess sin can do that to a person; spiritually blinding us so that we cannot see the error of our ways nor the dangers that they will lead to.

I discovered that he was cheating on me and that the girl was younger. I should have expected that he would have; I don't know why I didn't. I was dead set on revenge, but what was I to do now? Well, the only other thing I could: get another boyfriend (In Jamaica we would say *"bun him"*). I thought, "If he wants to cheat on me, then I will cheat on him; two can play this game." So, I moved on. I did eventually tell him that we were over, but sadly, he did not take me seriously.

My new boyfriend had his own business, and I wasn't afraid to drop in on him every now and again and pay him *that kind* of call. Unbeknownst to me, my previous boyfriend was keeping tabs on my movements, and he found out that I was seeing someone else. I eventually told him it was over.

The truth of it all is that sin begets more sin, and when our lives are void of Holy Spirit's influence, our spirituality will spiral downwards, taking our bodies and souls with it. King Saul's life is possibly one of the most telling of the biblical recounts which depicts the truth of this. One sin led to other acts of disobedience from which he was never able to recover: he didn't kill all the Amalekites as he was instructed by the Lord and blamed the people for the decision he made; he didn't wait on Samuel to perform the sacrifice; he tried to kill David; sought out a necromancer to call up Samuel's spirit; and he killed himself. It's like the Lord said, "...*if thou doest not well, sin lieth at the door." (See Genesis 4:7).*

The Lord is so surgical with His choice of words: *sin lieth.* The Hebrew word from which this was translated depicts sin as being in a crouching position, and Strong's states that it may also mean *recline, repose, brood, lurk or imbed.* The definition almost anthropomorphizes sin—it exhibits traits of something that is alive, like an animal ready to pounce on its prey and conducts itself in that manner. Can you imagine sin waiting on you to let it in, reclining by your door, or worse, lurking around to pounce on you at any minute? It is a living evil bringing a death blow (see Romans 6:23). Well, I was repeatedly pounced upon, but being spiritually blind, I could not have known. I was a carnal, natural woman. This is how Paul puts it in Romans 8:5-7:

"For they that are after the flesh do mind the things of the flesh; but they that are after the Spirit the things of the Spirit. For to be carnally minded is death; but to be spiritually minded is life and peace. Because the carnal mind is enmity against God: for it is not subject to the law of God, neither indeed can be."

The Lord's plan was and is never to have sin revisit and pounce upon me (nor you) at every turn. It is through knowing God that we understand what sin is, and until we know God, sin will forever be our portion, and forever be all that we know; that is never a good place to be in. As the scripture rightly said, *"Woe unto them that call evil good, and good evil; that put darkness for light, and light for darkness; that put bitter for sweet, and sweet for bitter!"* (Isaiah

5:20). I would soon find out even the more what these scriptures truly meant.

CHAPTER 4

SOUP! SOUP!

"**C**ould you take me to get some soup?" he asked. "I'm feeling sick, and I would like to drink some soup?"

"Ok, I'm coming for you." Of course, I had told him it was over, and I guess your question, the million-dollar question, would be "What in God's name was I doing trying to help him get soup?" Maybe I didn't think anything of the request and the softer side of who I was just would not allow me to refuse him the help he requested.

So, we bought the soup, and then we returned to his house. I drove into his yard and stopped at the end of his driveway, only to hear him say, much to my shock and amazement, "Me naah cum out!"[5]

"What!" I was curious and shocked but not traumatized; not yet anyway. I started to think about what he meant and what would become of my plans for the night. What would my date say when he came to pick me up and I was unavailable on account of

---

[5] "I'm not getting out!"

my "ex" threatening the success of it? "God, a wha' dis pon mi now?"[6]

As a means of persuading him to get out, I drove the car out of his driveway and to the end of the street, signalling that I was going to go about my business, regardless of his intentions, but that tactic did not work. So, as a last resort, a Hail Mary of sorts, I stopped the car and alighted from it, thinking that I would just leave him and go about my business—get to my date by some other means. But as fast as I could get out, he too came out, hurriedly ran around to the driver's side, held and shook me, and for want of a better word, *stuffed* me into passenger's seat via the driver's seat, and sat around the steering wheel.

It was now apparent to me that I wasn't going to make my date tonight.

"A wha dis mi get miself inna?"[7] I wasn't sure what would have ensued, but it felt all kinds of wrong. I remember the night so vividly. What was to transpire would forever haunt me, if it hadn't been for the Lord!

---

[6] "God, what is this now?"
[7] "What did I get myself into?"

"Yuh dis me!"[8] he said angrily, and at that point, I knew he had found out about the other companion. But this shouldn't have mattered; I had already told him it was over. Of course, I did not know how much he knew. "Who? It nah guh suh!"[9] In the rainy cold night, he found a secluded spot along our way to what should have been my doom, stopped the car, ripped and removed my underwear from under my denim off-the-shoulder dress, and proceeded to force himself on and into me. That was just the beginning, as miles down the road and many verbal exchanges later, my fate would become even clearer—as if being raped wasn't enough.

"God, nuh mek him kill me lef me two pickney dem,"[10] I said as we reached the end of the road.

"Come out a di car!!"[11]

God always has a plan for our lives, and it may seem farfetched or even impossible. How could He have a plan for every individual in a population of eight

---

[8] "You have disrespected me!"

[9] "Who? This is not how this is going to go!"

[10] "God, please don't let him kill me to leave my two children alone."

[11] "Get out of the car!!"

billion people? Well, if it were possible, by any human standard, to do this, then He would not be God. *"Our ways are not his ways, nor our thoughts his thoughts"* (Isaiah 55:9), and as much as we would like to pretend that we understand or even know how He thinks, we can never fathom His plan or ability. How do you fathom the power and ability of an individual who can do anything and everything? Beyond this, there are understandings that we have yet to grasp about our Creator. His plans for us may not be one of grandeur by our standards, but He has a way of giving honour to vessels of dishonour, which no one can subvert; not even the devils bound for hell.

As I stepped out of the car, the Lord showed up, and my captor began to have a panic attack. When I realized what was happening to him, I started my own intervention and started to utter soothing words, hoping to calm him down at least. I had to intervene, as surviving this ordeal was foremost in my mind. "Baby, wha' mek yuh a gwaan suh? Yuh luv me and me luv yuh. Mek wi just work it out nuh man?"[12] My words did not soothe or help him at all, but so debilitating was the panic attack that no strategy I

---

[12] "Baby, why are you acting like this? You love me and I love you. Why don't you let us just work it out?"

60

could conjure up could calm him down. I guess the Lord wasn't ready for him to be calm or functional just yet. The attack rendered him almost catatonic; I had to drive the car back home. Look at God!

Who else could it have been? This deliverance is a testament not to my goodness but to the fact that God wants to be on our side even when we aren't willing to be on His. But we MUST choose a side! In this battle of spirits, not choosing a side is also the same as choosing the wrong side. Can you imagine? Just a minute ago I was driven to my watery grave, and now I was trying to *resuscitate or revive*, as it were, my kidnapper, my killer-to-be. After the Lord calmed him somewhat, I bought him something to drink, and moments later, we were on our way back home.

It was at this moment that it all became a little bit less threatening and a bit more interesting. The other man in my life, the one who I had a date with, started calling my phone on our way back. You might have said that this shouldn't have been an issue; after all, even though my kidnapper was slowing regaining some composure, he was still in a bit of a panic; *it seemed as if we would work it out* (I only said those things because I didn't want to die, and for no other reason). The truth is, I told my date (the one I had that night) that I had parted ways with my "ex," the kidnapper, and my "ex" believed that he was going to be the only one, barring the fact that he might have found out about the date—a very ill-shaped "love" triangle, if I should say so. I couldn't let both know about each other; well, I couldn't let the one calling know about the ordeal, neither could I allow the one with me to confirm, even the more, what he might have already known.

"Ansa di phone!" He shouted at me as he seemingly was reviving from his panic-stricken state. I didn't answer the call. He got even more riled up, and while driving past a community in Vere, he yanked the emergency break (the devil's pathetic attempt to destroy me again), causing the car to spin uncontrollably in the road, colliding into a small embankment that separated the road from a gully— an almost sure death had we fallen into it. The car was immobile.

A stranger would come to our rescue. When we were asked what happened, like any *honest* Jamaican, we confessed outright: "A one dog run 'cross di road and we swing from it an' enup ya suh, enuh."[13] I guess

---

[13] "A dog ran across the road and we swung from it and collided with this embankment."

the safest thing was to blame it on the dog; after all, the dog wasn't going to tell. It was six o'clock the next morning when I closed the grill on my veranda, leaving him outside. I then revealed to him the torn underwear: "Me neva throw it away. Yuh rape me and mi a go mek yuh get lock up. Mi neva give yuh. Yuh tek it and rape me."

I didn't make my date.

NOT DESTROYED!

*A*bused. Raped. Threatened. Traumatized. Disobedient. Failed. Ignored. Self-willed. Promiscuous.

What more is there to say about who and what I was? I make no excuses for my past; I cannot. The Lord did not erase it from my memory either, but His love would prove to be all that I needed. I was always in love with the fellowship of God's people, thanks to my grandmother. I spent so much time with church people, and wherever they were I would find myself there. I guess my interest in the fellowship was always what He needed to get me where He wanted me to be and do what He wanted me to do.

CHAPTER 5

SALVATION AT LAST

"You coulda save?"

My peers and family members didn't believe that I would have gotten saved. Maybe they believed that I never could have; maybe I was their version of Mary Magdalene; I don't know, but I am inclined to agree. I was the talk of the town. I was always fashionably dressed, according to the standards of the day. When the time came, I dressed as freakishly as was legal; extremely short and tight attire, if you catch my drift; a rogue and rebel from the jump. I was partying all the time, and my lifestyle was untoward, to say the least. I guess that is why I love the Lord so much. His love and gift of salvation were unconditional towards me. Even while I was not saved and had quite a bit of baggage, He still took the time to minister to me. I was the one sheep He came searching for— *"What man of you, having an hundred sheep, if he lose one of them, doth not leave the ninety and nine in the wilderness, and go after that which is lost, until he find it?" (Luke 15:4).*

It would be convenient, even easy, for anyone to conclude also that having suffered through all the worldly and chaotic ordeals and having made it out alive, God favoured me. He had a calling on my life, and it was evident. No matter the kind of destruction the enemy had planned for me, the Lord was going to use them as steppingstones to victory. My tumultuous lifestyle and revelries had seen me giving birth, almost losing my life and soul, living lavishly, almost losing my life, living freely, almost losing my life, raped and cursed (Did I mention that I almost lost my life), but I was about to embark upon a journey, wherein His providence would be even more evident, and my steps would now be ordered by the Lord, Himself; a journey that would forever change my life.

"Saved, Saved, Saved"

Church was, and is, in my bones; my grandmother made sure of it. Every one of my strings, be it my umbilical cord, neck or heart string, rest assured, my grandmother would have seen to it that they were all cut, planted, germinated, and bore fruit at church: preparing my church clothes on Saturday, Sunday School, VBS, children's choir, listening to my grandmother pray for me and for all her children; I was *baptized* before I was baptized. I was trained in the way that my mother and grandmother wanted me to go—the way of the church—and I can certainly say that there is truth to Solomon's words after all.

I couldn't abandon the gathering together of the saints (see Hebrews 10:25). I guess there was some desire for the Lord regardless of how many times I slipped up or even if my heart was not His. As a matter of fact, I sought churches out. I found myself being drawn to so many different congregations and fellowships because of my early exposure, and one day I visited a prayer meeting in Mineral Heights that would seal my spiritual fate forever.

"If you go back out into that car without surrendering your life to Me this day," He said, **"You are going to die."** His words and voice were unquestionably distinct— *"Never man spake like this man"* (John 7:46)—and so was mine, as I wept bitterly and uncontrollably at His utterance.

"Yes, Lord!" I screamed at the top of my lungs. "Yes! Yes, I will! Yes! Baptize me now!" I shouted as my attention turned from responding to the Lord and to the congregants at the prayer meeting. "BAPTIZE ME NOW!"

Without any hesitation or delay, it was off to Salt River Pond from the small home in Mineral Heights—that home where the power of God was so evident, and His voice was so unmistakably clear.

God has a way of using the devil's plan to prove His power and unfold His purpose. The very same place where my life was almost snuffed out became the very place where I was reborn to life anew in Christ. The Most High was mocking the devil. I thank the Lord God for having a sense of humour (see Psalm 2:4). Instead of suffering a physical death, I suffered, yea embraced, my death to sin; instead of being led to the watery grave, I enjoyed a watery resurrection in Christ. Hallelujah!

My obedience to the voice of the Lord was met with a prophetic promise as I emerged from the depths of the pond: "Not many days hence, and you will be filled with the Holy Spirit, with evidence of speaking in tongues," Pastor Orr uttered as he completed the baptismal rite. So said, so done. That following Sunday, I was filled with the Holy Spirit and spoke in unknown heavenly tongues.

Ministry

Following my conversion, the Lord opened doors for me to minister with one Evangelist Carlton Daley. It was through ministering with him that the Lord opened my eyes to the ins and outs of deliverance ministry. I vividly recall that on one occasion, we were praying for a young lady who was incessantly fainting; she would fall or faint every minute after being revived. I hadn't seen anything like this before. While we were praying and calling on the Lord for her deliverance, someone came in and boldly requested that if we cannot deliver her, then we should all leave. When we heard it, we were utterly amused or maybe it was God's move in us, and we started laughing. It was at the sound of our laughter that the evil spirit left the young lady. The Lord always prepares you before sending you to work because it was ministering with Evangelist Daley that led me to minister in various parishes in Jamaica, a practice that I now wholeheartedly embrace.

This dimension of deliverance ministry was simply an addition to who I was. Even before I was saved, I was around the people of God. At one time, I spent two years working with the men and women of God. Even before those wonderful years of hearing God and working with His people, the Lord showed me favour and had been speaking into my life, making it abundantly clear that my life belonged to Him and that I should surrender. I also discovered the worshipper in me even then. While visiting different churches, I would immerse myself in worship. "Are you a Christian?" they would often ask.

On one life-defining occasion (okay, I have had a lot of life-defining occasions), being drawn into the presence of the people of God again, I attended an all-white fasting service being held by Bishop Richard A. McKenzie, my mentor and pastor who was jointly ministering to the congregation with Prophetess Loretta Sewell. The power of God was so evident, and many of the attendees were being slain in the Spirit. I was open to the encounter, but I made up my mind that I was not being slain in the Spirit that day. One of the ministers, aiding my mentor, anointed my feet and prayed for me and it was like any other prayer, but when Bishop McKenzie laid his hand on me, instead of being slain in the Spirit, I was hurled across the room. After I stood up, they said my face lit up like the sunshine being reflected by gold; they then testified that they had never seen the Lord do that to anyone before. This reminded me of Moses: *"And the children of Israel saw the face of Moses, that the skin of Moses' face shone"* (see

Exodus 34:29,30,35). Mind you, I was not saved at the time, but that didn't hinder God from showing me favour, again. I could not keep on running because every time I sinned or erred, I found myself crawling and clawing (I exaggerate) back to the Lord; convicted, as it were. The Holy Spirit's work was and is never done.

Besetting Sin and Breaking Free

I would have you understand, however, that God's plans for me were met with strong but subtle opposition. Wednesday, prior to being filled with the Holy Spirit, guess who paid me a "courtesy" phone call? Yes, my ex, the one who almost killed me. This was, most assuredly, my first trial—at least, I believed it was. I quickly confessed to him that I had taken my vows to serve the Lord and the life of unholiness was not for me anymore. "Me baptize!" I declared with an undertone of "*Me done! Yuh na get nuh more sex! Leave me alone. Gwaan bout yuh business.*"[14] If only I had uttered the undertone along with my actual statement.

---

[14] "I'm done! You will not be getting any more sexual favours from me. Go about your business."

I was "dead" months ago: spiritually, yes; physically, almost, but the Lord, here and now, had given me life; a life that I refused to let go. I didn't intend to revisit a sin-filled shell of an existence, and neither was I going to taste of its death, but I struggled to remain holy. Of a truth, the person who refrains from evil becomes "*a prey*" to perpetrators of evil (Isaiah 59:15a says, "*Yea, truth faileth; and he that departeth from evil maketh himself a prey*). I couldn't shake this man. My soul was knitted to him. Regardless of our separation and my salvation, he still thought he had a right to me, and I still felt connected to him. There was nothing that I would not do for him.

My body, like my heart and soul, on several occasions, became intertwined with his. I laid with him again and again, and the feeling of filth flooded my soul every time; it was like being fed rotting food. Yes, I felt like the fool of Proverbs 26:11 "*As a dog returneth to his vomit, so a fool returneth to his folly.*"

The idea of having one's soul tied to another comes from an understanding garnered from David and Jonathan's relationship.

"...the soul of Jonathan was knit to the soul of David." (1 Samuel 18:1).

Renee Allen Mckoy stated, which can also be easily assumed, that there are good and bad soul ties; this one between my ex and I would be the latter. Maybe, at that time, calling him my ex was a misnomer—we never left. The way I was tied to this man was more than just bad; it was deeply convoluted and spiritual. It was a prophetic word that revealed the unnatural, unholy bond that existed between us, all initiated, supported and fostered by witchcraft. What was I to do? I was saved, so why was I still bound? The bondage almost afforded me my life.

Having gone through that unforgettably traumatic experience, I would yet put myself in trouble with the same man. I got wind of his cheating escapades again; he was cheating with another woman who was younger than I was. I don't know why I thought he was having affairs with me alone. Why did I even care about his sex life or who he was dating? Wasn't I now saved? Even though I had slept with him again, weren't we on different pages? Anyway, I would not have it! I gave him my body even after I was saved, and now he was cheating on me? Yes, I was obsessed. I was bound. I was tied.

One day, when I finally caught up with him, I used my car and nudged his car. It didn't cause any damage to his car, but he was furious. He loved his car dearly, so, what better way to get back at him: "You hurt me, so I scratched your baby." I told you that I had made many mistakes. Well, this was shaping up to be one of the big ones. You would think that the near-death experience that God had to intervene and I had to talk my way out of would be engraved on my frontal lobe. What state of mind was I in, and why could I not think logically? I guess when you are tied to someone, all logic goes out the window or, should I say, windscreen, for no sooner than I had bumped his vehicle, he shot out the windscreen. "Not again?!"

This was not the life I wanted to lead, and after days and months of praying, the Lord freed me. Thanks be to God! When a calling is on your life, it is important that you do not allow it to linger over you unheeded. For me, it did, but the Lord says that He will have mercy on whom He will have mercy (see Exodus

33:19[15]; Romans 9:15[16]; Romans 9:18[17]). In the words of the classic Jamaican proverb, "puss and dog nuh have the same luck." This is not to say that God won't take the time to lead you into His presence, but the choice is always ours to make. One shattered windscreen, the threat of death, and whole heaps of prayer later, I am writing a book. *God is great and greatly to be praised* (see Psalm 48:1).

Humility

What makes my experiences more testimony-worthy is the fact that my past seemed to have meant nothing to the Lord because He treated me as if there were no errors in my life. He was not daunted or deterred by the fact that I had children out of wedlock. He was not repulsed by my scars and wounds; my disgrace did not dissuade Him from beginning or completing His work in me; despite my flaws, He still gave me a chance to represent Him. Despite my shortcomings,

---

[15] *And he said, I will make all my goodness pass before thee, and I will proclaim the name of the Lord before thee; and will be gracious to whom I will be gracious, and will shew mercy on whom I will shew mercy.*

[16] *For he saith to Moses, I will have mercy on whom I will have mercy, and I will have compassion on whom I will have compassion.*

[17] *Therefore hath he mercy on whom he will have mercy, and whom he will he hardeneth.*

He married me anyway (see Jeremiah 3:14). It is Christ who bought me so that I can say, like Fanny Crosby, "I am Thine, Oh Lord."

Destruction was not to become me.

You can already see that I wasn't ALL HOLY. I had and may still have flaws, which sadly reared their ugly heads in my church. I was gifted, anointed, and cocky. I started acting as if I knew more than my pastor, and what was worse, I did not listen to him. I did not submit to his authority, which the Bible encourages and provokes us to do. I became born again, but that little girl who loved to steal away to visit the beach was still very much alive. There was still rebellion in my heart, and God had to deal with me and apply His form of sandpaper to my rough edges. The scripture says two individuals who have not agreed on their path cannot walk together. I think that was who I was with my pastor and with the people around me; if I knew more than them and was more spiritual than they were, then I thought they could not and should not lead me. I was going to learn my lesson the hard way.

To add insult to my own self-inflicted injury (I speak of the rebellious nature within me), someone in the church told a lie on me. I couldn't disprove their claims, and as a result, I was stripped of my leadership positions. So, I had a decision to make. What do you do when you are caught between a rock of rebelliousness and cockiness and a hard place of public demotion and humiliation? You leave!

I left my church, but unfortunately, or possibly divinely ordered, I couldn't settle down in any other church. I became what Hugh Auchinloss calls a "church tramp"; not entirely, but some resemblance of one. Sadly, this "church-hopping" was a continuation of what I normally did while still a member of my own church. I was frequently absent from my church because I was attending another, and in that regard, I was rebellious. I had to learn, and now know, that this is an unacceptable practice. My dear friend and woman of God, Prophetess Loretta, who ministered to me years prior, told me to go back to my church. It took me months.

Before I returned, and without my knowledge, the Lord told my pastor to get me and tell me to moderate the service on my return, but I had a history that caused him to question the Lord's command in that regard. So, he placed a fleece before the Lord. "Lord, let me see a missed call from her if you want me to give her this duty," he prayed. God did better than that, much to my shame as well. The day he was expecting the text, I showed up at the church. When I showed up, the Lord told me to do the most humiliating and humbling thing that I had ever done. I showed up at the divine service, much to my pastor's amazement, and as instructed by the Lord, I went to the platform, knelt at my pastor's feet, apologized to him, and then I apologized to the entire congregation for my behaviour.

The Lord humbled me, but He also vindicated me as the Lord reinstated me into the leadership positions I had lost and promoted me as a minister as well. Lesson learnt—if I wouldn't willingly humble myself and be led by authority, the Lord will humble me Himself (see Luke 14:11[18]).

The Lord acknowledges leadership, and it is critical that we obey the leaders that the Lord has set above us to watch over us, for "...*rebellion is as the sin of witchcraft*" (1 Samuel 15:23a). When a saint of God is involved in the working of witchcraft, it makes the work of the Lord and the work of His servant that much harder. Our leaders should have our support so

---

[18] *For whosoever exalteth himself shall be abased; and he that humbleth himself shall be exalted*

that their work may be lighter, and we should all bear each other's loads (see Galatians 6:2) until the Lord returns. Of course, this does not mean there won't be disagreements, but our approach should be sprinkled with the right amount of humility.

The First Fruits of Favour

Many of the blessings I now enjoy come as a direct result of obedience to and faith in God; the Word is very clear about that. My unwillingness to yield to authority, and therefore to God, proved to be the blockages to my blessings. Of course, this is not always the case. There are always going to be trials of sorts that will cause one to question God's promises.

There were so many trials and situations that just did not bode well for me. I was doing a nine-to-five job and, to be fair, it wasn't the best of jobs, but I occupied myself nonetheless. I was working as an office attendant at a construction company's business office. On a regular basis, my utilities would get disconnected because of non-payment. One day a prayer partner of mine offered me some food (thanks be to God), but I didn't pay much attention to it, meaning, I cooked it and forgot to put it away in the fridge. Of course, it began to spoil (the early stages of spoilage; we call it *touch*). I warmed it and ate it (some would say that there is no shame in my game). I had nothing else to eat. It was the Lord who kept me because that was not the only incident where I had to look shame in the face, but again, for all those situations of shame, God came through.

A prophetic word of favour was spoken over my life by a Bishop: "You shall be receiving barrels from abroad," he said, and I welcomed that word with open arms. When you have had spoiled food, anything healthy and fresh is more than welcomed. This barrel-blessing continued up to this day to the point where these blessings have become the driving force behind my feeding program. One of my spiritual daughters, Thelma Martin, to whom I owe a debt of thanks, was moved by God to be a contributor to my feeding program for the poor, and thanks be to God, I have been visiting the wharf on several occasions to collect these barrels of food stuff.

CHAPTER 6

THE VERY FAITH OF GOD

As I went on my way, the Lord showed me His favour almost immediately. I was given an apartment to live in.

Much of the life I had while in sin was now gone, and it felt like we (my children and I) were going to start from scratch. At one point we had to move out of our house, and the Lord provided a ram in the thicket in the form of one of my prayer partners, Pastor Elaine Holness. There is a special love in my heart for her. For a year, my children and I slept on the same bed, and the space beneath the bed was our wardrobe. This woman of God who took us in was so good to us, giving up her best room to my children and I, and she fed us for the entire year; she taught me what it meant to give sacrificially.

During this time, I didn't know that I would be doing the same for others (giving sacrificially to fulfil their needs). Case in point, I took in a minister and her child when they were going through a rough time. I later extended the courtesy to another minister but for a much longer period. Such is the nature of the ministry to which I, WE, are called. Matthew states that *"...with what measure ye mete, it shall be measured to you again." (Matthew 7:2b).* Now I do not expect the same to be meted out to me, but the fact that I was a recipient of such love and kindness through this woman of God, I now do the same for as many as I can. What can I say, I believe the Word and the Writer without reservation.

Another woman of God from Canada approached me during my period of homelessness and told me to find an apartment and she would pay three-quarters of the rent; she did this for a year. I then had to move again, but all in all, the Lord was there. This journey led me to be more sacrificial in my giving. He blessed me so much that I was able to give away much of my furniture, which He later replaced. A pastor testified once that when he wanted a car, he went and washed the air outside his house as if he was washing his car, and I decided to use that very same kind of faith to pray a refrigerator into my life. I spoke to the spot where I wanted the new refrigerator and put out the old refrigerator, and the Lord provided a black stainless steel two-door refrigerator. All this is said simply to get you to understand that everything I have received was done by faith.

My daughter's academic accomplishments were better than mine, but I was not impressed with them, and no university would be either. She could have done much better, in my opinion. As a result, she was not eligible to attend university, so I had to weigh my options. She spent some time at home, of course, and I wasn't keen on her keeping that same kind of inertia—staying home doing nothing. *"Yuh too pretty fi stay home and duh nothing."* I had the same sentiments, in a manner of speaking, as my grandmother did. My intentions were to make sure that she became the best she could be.

Of course, this reminded me of my own life. I didn't get the motivation in high school, and I couldn't attend university. I was determined that my daughter would not suffer the same fate. She left high school with three subjects and was enrolled in another high school to re-sit the necessary subjects to make her eligible for university; she was not as successful there either. The sentiments of her being like her mother, not a naturally bright child, haunted me even more, but I was determined not to let that demotivate me.

In 2016, I went to the Northern Caribbean University and walked the campus, *decreeing* and declaring that my daughter would not just be enrolled as a student at that university but that she would complete her studies. GLORY TO GOD IN THE HIGHEST! My faith and work were met with victory, and in that very year, my daughter was enrolled.

There is something to be said about having the very faith of God. Even though it has been said, and even though this is the understanding that has been taught time and time again, and even though theologians have theologized it to the bone for ages, it is still worth mentioning; it is still worth uttering: we, the liberated, called of Christ, the faithful, should have the faith of God. When God performs an action or utters a word, He expects it to happen, and there can be no other outcome other than what He stated. If He states that a sea should be parted right now, He doesn't expect the sea to still be obeying its stated laws of physics. He is not expecting some gust of wind mightier than a category five hurricane to suddenly manifest and rip through the water even to the seabed. He is unconcerned with every other outcome; NO OTHER OUTCOME ENTERS THE MIND OF GOD; NO OTHER OUTCOME FINDS A PLACE IN HIS MIND. If other thoughts, other than the outcome which He states, enters His mind, then that would mean God doubts Himself, and GOD does not facilitate doubt. What He says, just is. As stated by Isaiah 55:11 - "*So shall my word be that goeth forth out of my mouth: it shall not return unto me void, but it shall accomplish that which I please, and it shall prosper in the thing whereto I sent it.*" In essence, therefore, much of God's faith is tied up in word and deed. I would like to believe that the Lord allowed me to function in that very same way with regards to my daughter's education; a practice I now perform in every area of my life.

My daughter's journey wasn't all smooth sailing though. She had to undertake a set of preliminary courses which would eventually qualify her for the course of study, and she struggled through some of her courses after qualifying. It would be no coincidence, therefore, given her background, that the field of Mathematics would have posed some sort of challenge; though not strange, it was anticipated. We, my prayer partners and I, spent hours on end praying that God would help her. In 2022, she became a proud graduate of NCU. Thanks be to God! I guess now I want her to be a bit more committed to Jesus; I still have faith.

"Manchester, here I come."

For two years, my daughter had to travel to NCU from May Pen, and living in May Pen was proving to be more difficult. On several occasions, I was behind on my rent, and the utilities would be disconnected from my house. My children sometimes went to school without lunch money, not often, but they made do. Other times, I simply acted on faith, and the Lord, like He always does, took care of all my needs. There were times when they went to school without money and the Lord would provide it right on time so I could deliver it to school for them.

A year prior, I had quit my job to become a full-time minister, and it was during that period I experienced these setbacks. An individual prophesied that my problems would be done away with if I moved to Manchester. I was not sure where to go, and I was also aware that living there would be expensive. Of course, I had no money to move, and I was uncertain of how it would all unfold. However, I left and made some calls. The Lord opened doors for an apartment, and I was blessed with the rent for an apartment, and the Lord ensured that all my bills were paid, and I was never without food.

The Lord has also blessed me to minister overseas, increasing my travelling. Every favour granted to me was on account of my actions of faith in God. What else could it have been? For years I had not travelled overseas, and the Lord, through Bishop McKenzie, prophesied into my life about ministering beyond the borders of Jamaica. "The Lord will open doors for you to travel to five Caribbean countries," and in that very year, the Lord paid my way to Trinidad and four other countries, and not a cent came out of my own pocket. The Lord sent me a destiny helper, a woman of God, to whom I also owe much gratitude. It was all in and for the glory of God.

The Cattle On A Thousand Hills

When we are wealthy, or think that we are wealthy, we show off our possessions, and so does God. The distinction is worth mentioning by far. A wealthy man shows off his cars, boats, houses, and bank accounts: the inanimate objects. God shows off the living things: His cattle, sheep, and PEOPLE. Notice how He phrases it in these scriptures: *"The earth is the Lords and the fullness thereof; the world, and they that dwell therein."* (Psalm 24:1). When was the last time you referred to a set of animals as THEY? Now consider Psalm 50:10-12: *"For every beast of the forest is mine, and the cattle upon a thousand hills. I know all the fowls of the mountains: and the wild beasts of the field are mine. If I were hungry, I would not tell thee: for the world is mine, and the fulness thereof.*"

God declares His wealth based on the things that are living, and no wonder He is a God of the living and not the dead (see Mark 12:27[19]). We are the ones who measure our wealth by the dead things around us: our beds, computers, and buildings. I can honestly say therefore that every good thing, every inanimate thing that has come into my life, has come through one of God's favour-designates: an ambassador for God's favour, if you will. For the first three or four years, my daughter's college tuition came directly from her father. In her final year, a few individuals pitched in and blessed us, and during the times when she had exams and we could not find the money, the accounting department granted us favour. Yes, FAVOUR—she sat her exams, and we paid when we had the money.

My grandfather (my mother's father) became one of those favour-designates. I told him I would like a piece of the land he owned. His initial statements were that one piece was for one of his daughters, and he intended on selling the other piece. So, that rested with me for a while, and then I made another request

---

[19] *He is not the God of the dead, but the God of the living:*

of him—yes, I still wanted a piece of the land, and to my surprise, he asked me "When do you want it?" At that point, I was thankful and ready to move forward with the acquisition. We did all the necessary paperwork, completed the survey, and we were well on the way to making the transfer. Subsequently, however, call it insatiable, call it a burden with the desire for more, I said to him "Why don't you just give me it all?" Can you believe it? He gave me the title; no questions asked.

The transfer needed to take place within a year, and the cost of the title transfer would be one hundred and forty-four thousand Jamaican dollars. I didn't have the money at all, but I made two payments through God's favour (I needed ninety percent for the process to begin), and while that was going on, I kept praying that God would preserve my grandfather's life long enough for us to complete the process. The process involved him writing a letter to the land authority to allow me to pick up the title for the land. It sounds a bit morbid, but my grandfather passed on just recently, but not before the transfer was complete. Not coincidentally, the Lord has spoken into my life that God was going to bless me with land (this prophetic word was uttered by Prophetess Loretta), and this land acquisition took place fifteen years after.

Without being anathematic, being given God's grace and favour goes hand in hand with patience, and patience, according to scripture, must have her perfect work in us (James 1:4[20]).

Healing in His Wings

Healing is my bread; doctors would suffer if I was their only patient. My illnesses and diseases are borne by Jesus Christ, for *"by his stripes [I am] healed"* (see Isaiah 53:5). The severity of these illnesses does not matter; I take them all to the Lord.

Even during the conversations and plans of writing this book, I was feeling a sharp pain in my lower back, almost in the region of my left kidney, and being the individual I am, I didn't hesitate to speak the word over this new omen which signalled some illness. As could be expected, the more I spoke words of healing and deliverance over this pain, the more excruciating it became. What could this mean? Well, consider this for a moment. Why would pain increase

---

[20] *But let patience have her perfect work, that ye may be perfect and entire, wanting nothing.*

92

given that you have spoken or have been speaking health over your life? Is this logical? Does God want you healed? This is a test of faith, if not directly, then indirectly. It is not easy to continue exercising faith while the pain and problems show no sign of abating. I adjure you, therefore, that you remain faithful in faith. Believe God to wit's end and speak life over your soul.

I continued to beseech the Lord saying, "God, You must heal me. I don't know where this is coming from and why I am in so much pain, but You must heal me." The more I besought the Lord for His healing, the more the pain grew. Later in the week, I had to join a prayer meeting and, even then, while I was in the prayer meeting, I was declaring my healing. I declared to everyone at the prayer meeting that I had been feeling a pain in my lower back, but testified, in faith, that God had healed me.

That declaration seemingly came too soon because immediately after, the pain grew more unbearable. I had finally had enough, laid my hand on my back, and declared authoritatively, "I curse this pain in the name of Jesus," and the pain left and has not returned since. Glory to God! It was God's decision to honour my declaration in faith that healed me, and I pray that you make the same choice—declare life in faith.

Countless Blessings From Acts Of Faith

The manner in which the remainder of this chapter unfolds is very dissimilar from previous chapters. There are just so many testimonies of the Lord's deliverance, and I will divulge them with as much grace as God gives me.

In the same breath, I recall saying to the Lord, after getting wet in the rain some time ago, that I really would like to have a car because I was tired of walking. Of course, like He always does, the Lord sent a word. Soon after that prophetic utterance, a friend of mine contacted me and told me they were in the process of purchasing a car. She said that I should keep it and take care of it.

The blessing continued beyond this. I remember the Lord instructed me to give my children's school money to another mother who was in need, and of course, I obeyed. My children were unable to go to school, but on the hinge of that obedience, the Lord sent me one hundred thousand Jamaican dollars

(JA$100,000); obedience is truly better than sacrifice (see 1 Samuel 15:22[21]).

Again, I was laid off from a particular company. When I first got the job, I sowed the pay cheque into the life of a woman of God. I was laid off for several months, but the Lord caused them to call me back to their job after some months, and my pay was substantially increased; an increase that amounted to the exact figure I was praying for during the time I was employed there. It does pay to sow because *"they that sow in tears [and in prayer, I might add] shall reap in joy" (see Psalm 126:5).*

Note that it was not all joy. There were days I would just yearn for a car; my experiences were fuelling my desires. I was preaching and doing the Lord's work, heading to anywhere the Lord would send me or open a door to minister but having to depend on public transportation and the uncertainty thereof was a bane to my travels. To attest to that fact, I was invited to minister in Santa Cruz (St. Elizabeth), and I hopped into a taxi and just went with the intention of

---

[21] *And Samuel said, Hath the Lord as great delight in burnt offerings and sacrifices, as in obeying the voice of the Lord? Behold, to obey is better than sacrifice, and to hearken than the fat of rams.*

returning home in the same manner. Some intention. As it turned out, I couldn't get a taxi. It took a stranger's mercy to get me back home. I was overjoyed that he would oblige me.

He drove a pickup truck with one long seat in the front carriage, so I hopped in. Sadly though, he began acting strangely, as much as I could derive. He had his phone resting between us, and he would ever so often take the phone up to look at it, all this time brushing my leg while doing so. Why would he do that, and he doesn't even know me? His action was a clear red flag, and I began to believe that this man had some ill intentions. I was on the Lord's assignments; if I had a car, I wouldn't be going through that. I prayed and asked the Lord to cover me for the entire duration of the drive back home. At one point, he stopped, and my fear and concern led me to pray even more. Thank God he came back to the vehicle and drove me straight to my hometown. It was pandemonium when I arrived home unscathed. I don't recall clearly who or when I got the confirmation of the man's intentions, but I was told that I had escaped a rape attempt.

I surely had my share of bad days, but this is what the journey is about. While I was in the world, I had the devil's blessing. My life looked really good to my eyes. When we become a child of God, there are battles to be fought before we see the blessings that the Lord has promised.

I can recall needing clothes to wear, and I could not afford some of the clothes I wanted. Instead of pining away at what I did not have, I went to the marketplace during the Christmas holidays and purchased second-hand clothing. Coincidentally, my choices were not bad because many of my friends saw me in these second-hand clothing and complimented me on my luck (like luck could have given me anything; a pity they didn't know what was going on), and like any child of God would do, I extended my appreciation. Many of the women around me loved the clothes I bought and wore and would ask me for them. I had no reservations in extending the hand of benevolence; I gave them whatever they asked for. I learnt to give sacrificial and giving away my clothes were a small sacrifice. The best part was, I understood what it was like not to have clothes, but these acts of kindness were seeds being sown. As a result, the Lord began to bless me with clothing, and the more He blessed me, the more I gave. Now, I have more items of clothing and shoes than I could ever need.

H.O.W. Come!

A couple of years ago, the Lord leveled the word of the plight of Christian women before me: women who were hurting and in need of healing; His instructions were very clear. It was time for me to reach out to these women; women like some of you reading this book; women who have been wearing their Christianity as a veil to cover the hurt they have been experiencing. The Lord told me that the hurting women in the church should be my priority, especially those who are married, simply because many of these women are wearing masks to cover their emotional scars; the mask of Christianity, concealing their pain and hurt from the church and the world.

When the Lord told me about this need that I must become a conduit for Him to address, I laboured in prayer over it for nine months (it was literally a baby); labouring over the word and vision until, finally, the Lord opened all the necessary doors. I had no money. I only had a vision, faith, prayer, and my Jesus; the four of us came into agreement. On May 06, 2017, the Lord (Yes, it was all His doing) held the first Healing Our Women Conference, and it was a success. Three hundred women attended the first installment, and many were healed of almost every

98

conceivable traumatically induced psychological problem: rape, molestation, divorce, suicidal thoughts, you name it. This has been the mark of the conference, and there was not a year when women were not healed or delivered.

One of my relatives told me that she was molested at a very tender age by a woman of the clergy, and it was at one staging of the conference that she revealed it. She was then in her mid-fifties. *It is never too late for deliverance.* Two very distinct instances that stood out to me had to do with two females who had been molested by a pastor and an evangelist respectively. They have been living with the trauma for quite some time. In the second case (the case of the evangelist), the ordeal took place at the early and delicate age of twelve years; they were also healed and set free.

Physical healings also mark these God-ordained convenings. One of our ministers, Bishop Haber, came to minister, and at the time, she was wearing a large bandage around her belly courtesy of getting burnt. The Lord healed her instantaneously. During the 2022 staging, women were healed during worship, and there was one woman online who stated that God delivered her from several issues while she was listening and praising the Lord incessantly throughout the session. The Lord, like the Strategist that He is, has been taking care of all expenses: the ministers, musicians, décor, and He did what He said He would do: heal the women. What a GOD!

The conference has since been held every year, with the exception of one of the years of lockdown because of COVID-19, and it has been at no charge to any of the attendees. To mobilize individuals and provide food for the attendees is not a small feat in my mind, but there is no year where the Lord has not provided the funding for food, honorarium for ministers who are based locally and abroad, rental fee for venue and seating, sound equipment and re-enforcement and much more. Every dime was provisioned by the Most High, and not one year has the conference been in the red.

Giving To The Poor

There are some scriptures in the New Testament that demonstrates Jesus Christ's sentimentality and feelings for us. In Matthew 9:36, He was moved with compassion when He saw the multitude who were faint and lacked leadership. He was moved with compassion to the point of healing the sick in Matthew 14:14. He was moved with compassion when the leper cried out for help (see Mark 1:41). There is a myriad of people all over the world who are homeless and in need of food; Jamaica is no exception. The Lord has therefore allowed me the privilege to walk in the footsteps of Jesus and possibly feel the same kind of compassion that Jesus had for those in His day. You will note that the scriptures state that it was when He saw the multitude of people; it was the vast number of people who were suffering that moved Him. What say we as Christians?

I believe the Lord has moved me with compassion for the poor. Much of what I have, have always been used to feed and clothe the impoverished of our society. I believe that churches should revisit this ministry wholeheartedly and begin, again, to show compassion for the less fortunate among us. We are the body of Christ, and therefore our hands must reach out to the poor and destitute among us; we must breach our walls and find these people wherever they are. It is through my desire to feed the poor that barrels have not stopped coming to me. The Lord opens doors for me to be a conduit for these poor, malnourished people who are in need of love and salvation but are also in dire need of food and nurturing. If the Lord had the poor on His heart from the beginning of time, how can we do less? Here is what the Lord says:

- If there be among you a poor man of one of thy brethren within any of thy gates in thy land which the Lord thy God giveth thee, thou shalt not harden thine heart, nor shut thine hand from thy poor brother. (Deuteronomy 15:7).

- He hath dispersed, he hath given to the poor; his righteousness endureth for ever; his horn shall be exalted with honour. (Psalm 112:9).

- He that hath pity upon the poor lendeth unto the Lord; and that which he hath given will he pay him again. (Proverbs 19:17).

- He that hath a bountiful eye shall be blessed; for he giveth of his bread to the poor. (Proverbs 22:9).

- He that giveth unto the poor shall not lack: but he that hideth his eyes shall have many a curse. (Proverbs 28:27).

- Jesus said unto him, "If thou wilt be perfect, go and sell that thou hast, and give to the poor, and thou shalt have treasure in heaven: and come and follow me." (Matthew 19:21).

(Even though this was a test, you can see the difference between Jesus' heart and the rich young ruler. Those of us who do have it all, even a strong sense of righteousness, may still not have a giving heart.)

It is my belief that the blessings I am now experiencing in God are a direct result of my decision to feed the poor. It is now, and will continue to be, my prayer that all saints, everywhere, extend their hands, the hands that Jesus Christ has given to us, the hands that should be extensions of His, to the people who need it most: the poorest among us. It is time for us to have a passion for those who are less fortunate: the widows and children in need.

Favour In Battle

I end this chapter with the sound of victory from battles of another front.

In 2017, I had a horrifying dream. A tall black man visited me and told me unquestionably that I was going to die, and it was in that year I experienced several bouts of attacks from the enemy. So gruesome were these attacks that they plagued my health. I began to lose weight, and I was very fearful about what was happening to me. Sad to say, again, many persons began to question me about it, and I was so embarrassed and even now am, but I said that that it was because of my new turmeric drink diet. Fact is, I couldn't put my finger on this situation, and being that I was not one to frequent the doctor's office, it was just a matter of trusting God. So, I prayed, and prayed, and prayed. What else could I do? Who else did I have? Where else could I go? My constant prayer was my way of looking to the hills; *It's the only way to look to the hills*. It was while I prayed and sought the Lord that the Lord gave Psalm 23 to me, and it never left my lips.

During that time, my mirror and I became very close acquaintances. Whenever I could, I would gaze into it and, while doing so, I would anoint myself and speak life into my own body: "I shall not die but live and declare the works of the Lord," I uttered. "Yea though I walk through the valley of the shadow of death, I will fear no evil." It was a year later when the Lord completely delivered me. God's salvation goes hand in hand with healing and deliverance, no matter what anyone else says.

With every bit of favour God granted to me, more of my life had to be committed to Him. How did I show that commitment? I did His bidding. During the pandemic, I had to make the gospel known in the highways and byways, and Jesus showed up at every turn. Women were saved and delivered, and to God alone be the glory. Like Peter and John, being whipped by COVID-19 was the least of my problems (I've had my fair share), so preaching the gospel in marketplaces and on street corners is the least I could do for the One who has granted me such favour.

CHAPTER 7

FORGIVENESS, FAITH, AND FAVOUR

"We are not exempted from pain. Even if we do not cause it ourselves, we will undoubtedly experience it at the hand of something or someone else. But God will grant us favour – peace in the midst of the storm or He will speak peace to the winds." —Leo Lewis

The Lord, and my decisions, have positioned me to identify with many hurting women. I have tasted trauma and truth, pain and pleasure, lust and love, and humour and heartache. My life was an emotional roller-coaster, much like the women I have had the pleasure and privilege of ministering to for my Lord, and like Paul, I can also say "*I know both how to be abased, and I know how to abound: everywhere and in all things I am instructed both to be full and to be hungry, both to abound and to suffer need.*" (Philippians 4:12). My life is the epitome of 2 Corinthians 4:8-9: "[I am] *troubled on every side, yet not distressed*; [I am] *perplexed, but not in despair; Persecuted, but not forsaken; cast down, but not destroyed.*" (emphasis mine). Therefore, my heart is extended to you.

I know what you have felt, or might have been feeling, because I am acquainted with suffering. Many of my past tribulations have not been mentioned in this book; however, from the many lines you have already read, you can see where I was and what the Lord had to deliver me from. I am aware of what it means to be told that "*you will amount to nothing*" (recall my grandfather), and I know the kind of psyche that such utterances will create. If your family rejects you or you feel rejected for some reason, then you will seek validation elsewhere, and this can make you vulnerable. However, like Jesus, our reactions must be "*Father, forgive them, for they know not what they do.*" (Luke 23:34). Because we (women) are more susceptible to feeling hurt, it is incumbent upon us as women to live lives of forgiveness or we will become wells of bitter water even though professing Christians, and a well cannot, or in our case, should not produce bitter and sweet water (see James 3:11).

I understand what it is like to be vindictive and vengeful. I followed my ex for a while after experiencing the feeling of being betrayed and slighted. After suffering such hurt, the only thing that might occupy your mind is the hurt, and you might feel the inclination to revenge that pain. Without question, the devil will seek an occasion to torment you with this thought, but let forgiveness be your revenge because, as you would have read, my pursuit for revenge almost cost me my life. Vengeance belongs to the Lord, and He will repay (see Romans 12:19). I would have been the headlines of the local news program if it hadn't been for God's protection.

As women, we must learn to let go and let God. Our ability, or willingness, to forgive comes with an irrevocable promise from the Lord: *"If you forgive, then I'll forgive you"* (see Matthew 6:15). I would believe that being unforgiving is not worth the fires of hell, and if for some reason we are unable to forgive, then we should take the posture of the man in Mark 9:24 and fashion our prayer in the very same way: *"Lord, I forgive; help Thou my unforgiveness."*

Often, it is not a matter of what we must do or be but what we should allow God to do or be in us. I recall at one point after my conversion, one of the individuals who hurt me got badly injured, and for some reason, I felt nothing: no compassion, no sorrow, nothing. I was surprised at the state of my heart, and after some self-examination, I realized that unforgiveness had been the root of my callousness. I chose, at that moment, to reach out to him and tell him clearly and whole-heartedly that I had forgiven him for all he did to me and requested that he forgive me for whatever hurt I had dealt him. Thereafter, I wept, but as the Lord promised, as a result of my action of forgiveness, a weight was removed from me; the weight of unforgiveness. It is like the story of the rich ruler forgiving a man of a huge debt. I guess a huge debt was removed from my back as well. Forgiveness, like any other sin, is a weight, and that is why Jesus implored us, according to Mark 11:25: "*And when ye stand praying, forgive, if ye have ought against any: that your Father also which is in heaven may forgive you your trespasses.*" In forgiving, we truly become like the Lord of whom the psalmist wrote in Psalm 86:5 - "*For thou, Lord, art good, and ready to forgive; and plenteous in mercy unto all them that call upon thee.*" If our Creator is forgiving; should we not also be forgiving?

The devil intends for us to get bitter with every trial, and to some extent, you may be persuaded that you have the right to feel bitter about what happened to you. If your ordeal made you bitter, then neither will you win against the pain that you are feeling. We cannot be the monkey gripping the fruit inside the bottle while still panting for freedom. We must choose freedom and not the fruit of unforgiveness.

If you are not saved, or a Christian, then you are trying to fight this battle of life by yourself, and you don't have to. As a matter of fact, you do not have the spiritual tools. God has enabled us as Christians, all who are willing to accept the gift of salvation, to fight the things which are not holy. The devil would want to use your hurt to plant seeds of ill-will, but "...all things work together for good to them that love God, to them who are the called according to his purpose." (Romans 8:28). Our tests become testimonies that form pathways and roads to help others on their own journey. Like Shadrach, Meshach, and Abednego, you are not just fireproof; the Firewalker is there with you; the Firewalker is walking around with you in the furnace; "The Lord of hosts is with [you]; the God of Jacob is [Your] refuge." (Psalm 46:7 – emphasis mine).

The Lord's promises are ever true, and you should take His counsel and not your own. Therefore, when you are going through the water, the Lord promises to be with you. Your trials are just there to try your substance. The fire will not burn you, nor will the water overflow you. Being crushed is part of the preparation. There is better ahead of you, and this process is preparing you to receive and become a better steward of God's gifts and calling on your life.

So, you will come out as pure gold. I did, and I still am. Why should my experience with God be different from yours? After all, the Lord is no respecter of persons (see Acts 10:34), and therefore if I can rejoice in the victory that He has given to me, then your victory is most assuredly ahead of you, if you will hold His hand in faith. Haggai 2:9 is for you in this regard: your latter state will be greater than your former because His thoughts are thoughts to prosper you (see Jeremiah 29:11).

After you have fully allowed the Lord's forgiveness to take hold of you, then having faith will be the next hurdle. As Hebrews declares, it is through the hearing of the word that one's faith is established, and as we already know, it is only through faith that we can even remotely begin to please God (see Hebrews 11:6). The way the scriptures arrive, or even determine the precept, is also critical because he who comes to the Lord must first believe that *He is*, and secondly, believe that *He is a rewarder of those who diligently seek him*. It is by faith we approach the Most High because "*no man hath seen God at any time*" (see John 1:18, John 6:46, 1 John 4:12). To get a word from God is not simply a statement that suggests that you should actively seek out the prophetic. What it means is that you should ever endeavour to hear from God for yourself. Whether it is Him speaking to you directly or through the scriptures, and upon receiving said word, it is what you will now hold dearest to your heart, believing in God for its fulfilment.

Notice the way I have just laid this concept out: it begins with a word, then a belief. God uttered a word about my conference for hurting women, and it was by faith that all the elements thereof coalesced. Every victory in my life started with a word that I then watered with faith and prayer. That therefore is the understanding I wish to leave with you: get a word from God and then act by faith. Now this word may not be prophetic. As a matter of fact, the scriptures form the basis for all prophetic utterances. So, get a word from the Word. As a matter of fact, get every word from the Word.

It is with faith we endure, so that we may come out as pure gold. I could go on to talk about the nature of gold and the process of purification, but a more exciting metaphor is worth mentioning here. Very early makers of wine had to crush the grapes to release the juice. Of course, in the days before modern ways of preparation were developed, grapes were crushed and fermented in huge barrels. The grapes were picked and placed in this large tub-like wooden structure. Women were then employed to walk around on these grapes with their bare feet until all the juice came out. When you are enduring, sometimes it feels like you are being crushed under someone's feet. You feel low and beneath it all, and the action hurts even to the point of you giving up your juice (your substance). As hard as it may seem, try to consider this crushing as part of the process; a process that you have yielded yourself to; a process that the Lord will turn around for your good.

Let's be fully aware that these are God's plans, and they may never come to fruition if we do not play our part. We will not experience God's favour if we do not have faith. Henceforth, our path, whether we understand it or not, comes with God's plan firmly and solidly defined: Forgiveness, Faith, and Favour. To forgive, remember that you are not infallible, and if God can forgive how much you have hurt Him, why can you not forgive your brother? And, yes, we have hurt the Lord. Every act of sin is an insult and a slap across the Lord's face, but He forgives us. *"Physician, heal thyself"* by forgiving those who have hurt you. *"Have the very faith of God"* to the fulfilment of His Word in your life. Thank Him for the favour that is about to come your way because you have done the first two steps.

Do not think that my journey was easy; you have seen from previous chapters that it wasn't. I attribute my successes and victories to staying in God, whether that meant staying in church or keeping my hope firmly in the Lord. I would often fall, but I got back up (see Proverbs 24:16); that is how I know I was marked for the Kingdom of God. Maybe you don't think the way I think, and maybe you have fallen on several occasions; some of you may just have fallen and decided to pick this book up. It is imperative that you understand: you do not have to think like me, nor do you need to have all the self-same experiences I had. What is critical, beyond your failures and flaws, is that you get back up. Destruction befalls those who stay down. Get up with your bruises and scars and walk again. Get up in your battered state and put one foot before the other again. If you are depressed, you can still walk. If you are oppressed, you can still walk, even if you are limping along. Victory is ahead though hard the road.

"For a just man falleth seven times, and riseth up again." (Proverbs 24:16a).

Damaged woman, will you get up like I did?

EPILOGUE

Our faith, I believe, is just an extension of God's faith. He is the one who has unlimited faith, so when we believe in Him, our faith becomes the passengers of His faith.

AUTHOR BIOGRAPHY

 Julene Grant-Percy is an ordained Apostle in her church circle and has been ministering the gospel of Christ in Jamaica for years. She ministers wherever she is requested, and is passionate about evangelising, after all, "He who wins soul is wise." Christ's ministry through her extends beyond preaching as she finds opportunities to feed the street people of her hometown. For the past three years, the Lord has helped her to organise the Healing Our Women conference, which has the purpose of bringing women to the Lord so they may be helped, healed, and delivered from trauma associated with devastating and debilitating experiences. Apostle Julene Grant-Percy is the mother of two children: Cristiano and Chenelle Tomlinson.

REFERENCES

1. Dickens, Charles. 1859. A Tale of Two Cities.

2. The Gleaner Company. 2022. Past winners of ISSA/GraceKennedy Boys' and Girls' Championships. 5 April. Accessed July 22, 2022. https://jamaica-gleaner.com/article/sports/20220405/past-winners-issagracekennedy-boys-and-girls-championships.

Made in the USA
Columbia, SC
26 February 2024

32041474R00067